Playing with Plays™
Presents
Shakespeare's

A Midsummer Night's Dream
FOR KIDS

(The melodramatic version!)

For 9-20+ actors, or kids of all ages who want to have fun!
Creatively modified by Brendan P. Kelso
Cover illustrated by Shana Lopez
Edited by Hannah Sidaris-Green

3 Melodramatic Modifications to Shakespeare's Play
for 3 different group sizes:

9-10+

11-14+

15-20+

Table Of Contents

To Cherice;
without her support, dedication, and drive,
I would not have gone this far!

And to the kids who perform,
you make all of this worthwhile!

-Brendan

Foreword

When I was in high school there was something about Shakespeare that appealed to me. Not that I understood it mind you, but there were clear scenes and images that always stood out in my mind. Romeo & Juliet, "Romeo, Romeo; wherefore art thou Romeo?"; Julius Caesar, "Et tu Brute"; Macbeth, "Double, Double, toil and trouble"; Hamlet, "to be or not to be"; A Midsummer Night's Dream, all I remember about this was a wickedly cool fairy and something about a guy turning into a donkey that I thought was pretty funny. It was not until I started analyzing Shakespeare's plays as an actor that I realized one very important thing, I still didn't understand them. Seriously though, it's tough enough for adults, let alone kids. Then it hit me, why don't I make a version that kids could perform, but make it easy for them to understand with a splash of Shakespeare lingo mixed in? And viola! A melodramatic masterpiece was created!

The entire purpose of this book is to instill the love of acting and Shakespeare into kids. I initially wrote my first Shakespeare play (Hamlet) to teach a few kids how to have fun with Shakespeare. It has evolved into a revolving door of new and returning kids constantly wanting more and more Shakespeare, from kids asking for the entire Shakespeare anthology for Christmas to writing a report in their 2nd grade class on heroes and choosing Shakespeare. Shakespeare is difficult enough when you are an adult, let alone a teenager (I didn't have a clue what Julius Caeser was about, except for "Et tu Brute!"). But for kids, most people (those calling themselves "adults" mind you) told me to forget it, "you can't teach kids Shakespeare". Well, I will have you know, that not only do these kids love Shakespeare now, they want more of it! And when you have children who have a passion for something, they will start to teach themselves, with or without school.

THE PLAYS: There are 3 plays within this book, for three different group sizes. The reason: to allow educators or parents to get the story across to their children regardless of the size of their group. Experienced actor variation: If you read any Shakespeare play as an actor you will notice one very common occurrence – NO STAGE DIRECTIONS. Okay, it happens occasionally, but it's very rare. Any actor with creative skills will tell you that this is a wonderful thing: it leaves full interpretation to the actor. Therefore, for the children who wish to explore their creative side, I suggest taking the play and whiting out ALL of the stage directions, allowing for the more experienced actors to be as creative as they want to be.

These plays are intended for pure fun. Please DO NOT have the kids learn these lines verbatim, that would be a complete waste of creativity. But do have them basically know their lines and improvise wherever they want as long as it pertains to telling the story, because that is the goal of an actor: to tell the story. In A Midsummer Night's Dream, I once had a student playing Quince question me about one of her lines, "but in the actual story, didn't the Mechanicals state that 'they would hang us'?" I thought for a second and realized that she had read the story with her mom, and she was right. So I let her add the line she wanted and it added that much more fun, it made the play theirs. I have had kids throw water on the audience, run around the audience, sit in the audience, lose their pumpkin pants (size 30 around a size 15 doesn't work very well, but makes for some great humor!) and most importantly, die all over the stage. The kids love it.

I have a basic formula that I use for these plays:
Day 1: I perform my own solo 5-minute Shakespeare play (I am totally winded by the end of it, because I have been all over the set and have died a few times if I can fit it in); we all read through the play together (randomly handing out parts); then auditions – and all auditions MUST include the actors best dieing scenes (they love this the most and will line up again and again to die on stage); the other is for the screams, they love this too, but don't forget to bring earplugs, they will be incredibly loud for both girls and boys since not all have come of age yet.
Day 2: Parts are given out; we read through the play again with our new parts; start blocking
Day 3: finish blocking; rehearse
Day 4: rehearse-no scripts
Day 5: rehearse; try on costumes, and dress rehearsal
Day 6: 2 Dress rehearsals and then performance.
This can easily be stretched to an 8 day course with the 2 extra days used for more rehearsal; set design; invitation creation; makeup practice; etc. As any director will tell you, actors can always use more rehearsal.

THE BARD'S WORK: As you read through the plays, there are several lines that are highlighted. These are actual lines from Shakespeare's text. I am a little more particular about the kids saying these lines verbatim. We need to do these correctly because we don't want to upset Willie. I find that there are many benefits to having these lines in there:

1. Kids are so cute when they are spouting Shakespeare.
2. Parents love to know that their kids are learning actual Shakespeare verbiage.
3. Most lines are very famous lines that they will come across later in life (to be or not to be; Romeo, Romeo, wherefore art thou; double, double toil and trouble; etc.)
4. The kids tend to feel they are more important when they are saying Shakespeare's lines.
5. The lines are easy to understand, giving the kids confidence that they will understand more Shakespeare lines later in life.

One last note: if you loved our plays, want to tell the world how much your kids loved performing Shakespeare, or are just a fan of Shakespeare, then hop on our website and have fun:

PlayingWithPlays.com

Oh yeah, and don't forget to sign up on our mailing list (emails rarely happen anyway) and we will give you insider information on new launches, book signings, speaking engagements, and some cool book discounts!

With these notes I bid you adieu, have fun, and good luck!

The 10-Minute or so
A Midsummer Night's Dream
By William Shakespeare
Creatively edited by Brendan P. Kelso

9-10+ Actors

CAST OF CHARACTERS:

HERMIA – Daughter of Egeus and in love with Lysander

LYSANDER – In love with Hermia

HELENA – In love with Demetrius

DEMETRIUS – Thinks he is in love with Helena

OBERON – King of the Fairies

PUCK – Troublemaker fairy - works for Oberon

TITANIA – Queen of the Fairies

*****QUINCE** – Leader of the Mechanicals

BOTTOM – Lead actor of the Mechanicals

FLUTE – An actor in the Mechanicals

****MECHANICALS** – a group of crazy actors

*Quince can be deleted from play if there are only 9 actors, just follow script notes.

**Mechanicals can be extra characters if needed.

ACT 1 SCENE 1

HERMIA: Oh .... LYSANDER!!!!! *(LYSANDER enters)*

LYSANDER: What's wrong, Hermia?

HERMIA: The Duke said I have three choices: execution, go to a nunnery, or listen to my father.

LYSANDER: Why?

HERMIA: My dad wants me to marry Demetrius, bleh...., but I want to marry you, Lysander!

LYSANDER: That's all right, Hermia. The course of true love never did run smooth. We'll run off to my Aunt's house. She lives in a place that is far, far, far away and we will go through an enchanted forest in the middle of the night and probably get lost!

HERMIA: Sounds great! *(HELENA enters)*

HELENA: *(depressed)* Oh Hermia, Demetrius loves your beauty. Why can't I be hot like you, then maybe he would love my beauty!

HERMIA: Wow, stinks to be you. Hey, want to know a secret?

HELENA: Yeah!

HERMIA: *(as if whispering in her ear)* Lysander and I are going to run off to his Aunt's house. It's far, far, far away. Promise me you will not tell a single person!

HELENA: Promise! *(HERMIA and LYSANDER exit)* *(To audience)* Hmmmm....I have a better idea, why don't I let Demetrius know of fair Hermia's flight, and then maybe he will fall in love with me!

(HELENA exits)

ACT 1 SCENE 2

(QUINCE, BOTTOM, and FLUTE enter)

QUINCE (or delete line): Is all our company here?

BOTTOM: FLUTE!!!

FLUTE: What?

BOTTOM: Listen here, Quince, our fabulous director, wants us to perform a play for the Duke and Duchess.

QUINCE (or FLUTE): Great! How about this one, *(takes script from BOTTOM'S hand)* 'The most lamentable comedy, and most cruel death of Pyramus and Thisbe', and we shall call it...... "Pyramus and Thisbe".

BOTTOM: Exactly!

QUINCE (or FLUTE): Great! You play the lead part, Pyramus!

BOTTOM: No, No, No! That's not acceptable! I deserve the best part because I am the best actor!

FLUTE: *(To audience)* More like OVERactor.

BOTTOM: I heard that. *(glaring at Flute)*

QUINCE (or FLUTE): That is the best part.

BOTTOM: Oh, well then.

QUINCE (or BOTTOM): Flute, you will play Thisbe.

FLUTE: *(spoken in a very manly voice)* Great! What is Thisbe? A wandering knight?

QUINCE (or BOTTOM): *(snickering to himself)* No, *she* is the lead female part, and you can talk in a small voice.

FLUTE: What?! Did I hear you right? Let me not play a woman; I have a beard coming.

BOTTOM: Fine, let me play Thisbe too!

(starts acting like a girl)

QUINCE (or FLUTE): No. You already have a part, the best part.

BOTTOM: Yeah, yeah.

FLUTE: Do I have to play a girl? This is not good, not good at all. *(all exit)*

ACT 2 SCENE 1

(PUCK enters)

PUCK: *(to audience)* Just want you all to know that I am a shrewd and knavish sprite call'd Puck. I cause all sorts of trouble. Sometimes I can be a devilish little imp. Yep. That would be me! *(very proud)* Oh look, here comes Titania, Queen of the Fairies, and look over there, it's Oberon, King of the Fairies. He's my boss.

(OBERON and TITANIA enter)

OBERON: *(Rude and sarcastic)* Hello.

TITANIA: Goodbye. *(Just as rude and sarcastic, and wanting to leave in a hurry)*

OBERON: Wait, please, there is something that I would like to tell you.

TITANIA: What?

OBERON: *(in a sing-song voice)* I don't like you!

TITANIA: *(heavy sarcasim)* Boo hoo, boo hoo hoo.

OBERON: If you give me the treasure I asked for, then I will go with thee.

TITANIA: Not a chance. I'm out of here!

OBERON: *(mocking TITANIA)* I'm out of here!

TITANIA: Bye bye! *(TITANIA exits)*

OBERON: *(very mad)* AAAAGGGGGHHHHH!!!!!!!!! I have to do something mean to her! *(talking to himself)* What to do? What to do? What to do?

PUCK: *(with a big grin)* So, how can I help?

OBERON: Go get me the magical purple flower.

PUCK: I'll put a girdle round about the earth in forty minutes. *(PUCK starts to leave)*

OBERON: Huh? *(not understanding what Puck just said)*

PUCK: *(frustrated)* I'll be right back. *(shaking his head and mumbling, PUCK exits)*

(HELENA and DEMETRIUS enter. OBERON watches, unseen)

DEMETRIUS: I love thee not, therefore pursue me not.

HELENA: Demetrius, don't you love me?

DEMETRIUS: No, you bug me, Helena.

HELENA: Even though I told you about Hermia and Lysander running off together?

DEMETRIUS: You still bug me. Now leave me alone... *(shoves HELENA away)*

HELENA: Demetrius, the more you hate me, the more I will love you!

DEMETRIUS: Aghhhhh! Leave me alone! *(HELENA chases DEMETRIUS offstage. PUCK enters)*

PUCK: Your fairy has returned with the magical purple flower!

OBERON: I pray thee, give it me. *(PUCK hands the flower to OBERON)* This is a love potion. I'm going to put some on Titania's eyes. Then she will awake and fall in love with the first thing she sees, hopefully something filthy and smelly! Puck, you go do something constructive.

PUCK: Constructive?

OBERON: *(frustrated)* I saw a young Athenian couple mad at each other. Use this flower and make them fall in love.

PUCK: Okay! *(PUCK exits. OBERON hides behind a tree)*

ACT 2 SCENE 2

(TITANIA enters)

TITANIA: Wow, I'm tired. I think I will fall asleep in the middle of this dark and enchanted forest, while my husband is very, very mad at me.

(TITANIA falls asleep)

OBERON: Well, well, well, looky here! *(OBERON, places potion on TITANIA'S eyes)* Wake when some vile thing is near! *(OBERON exits)*

(LYSANDER and HERMIA enter)

LYSANDER: Hmmm, these trees look familiar.

HERMIA: What do you mean by that?

LYSANDER: I have forgot our way.

HERMIA: That's okay. I'm tired. Let's go to sleep.

LYSANDER: Okay. *(LYSANDER and HERMIA lie down and go to sleep)*

PUCK: *(PUCK enters and sees LYSANDER lying on ground)* An Athenian couple, just like the boss said! Pretty soul, how can he be mad at her? A little on each eye and poof, you will now fall in love with the first thing you see! *(places potion on LYSANDER'S eyes. PUCK stands back to watch)*

(DEMETRIUS and HELENA enter)

DEMETRIUS: You are still annoying me, you're like my dog.

HELENA: Then let me be your pet and I will follow you everywhere. *(howls with excitement)*

DEMETRIUS: Nooooo! Hey, look at that *(points at something off stage in opposite direction, HELENA looks)* I'm outta here! *(DEMETRIUS exits)*

HELENA: Aghhhh *(Sees LYSANDER lying on ground, wakes him)* Lysander? Lysander, if you live, good sir, awake. *(HELENA kicks LYSANDER)* I said AWAKE!

LYSANDER: What? *(LYSANDER wakes up totally in love with Helena)*

HELENA: I think Demetrius does not love me.

LYSANDER: And run through fire I will for thy sweet sake.

HELENA: Huh?

LYSANDER: I love you!

HELENA: *(very matter of fact)* But you love Hermia.

LYSANDER: Not Hermia, but Helena I love: Who would not change a raven for a dove? *(Chasing her, trying to hug and kiss her)* Oh kiss me darling!

HELENA: Aghhhhhhhhh! *(HELENA screaming runs off stage, LYSANDER chases her)*

(HERMIA wakes up, confused)

HERMIA: Hello? Lysander? Where did you go? *(HERMIA exits other side. PUCK is very amused with the situation)*

ACT 3 SCENE 1

(QUINCE, BOTTOM, and FLUTE enter. PUCK is excited that there are new people to watch)

BOTTOM: There are some lines that I think we need to change in the script.

QUINCE (or FLUTE): No, we need to rehearse.

BOTTOM: Okay, I need to warm up first. *(BOTTOM moves over to the side of the stage to "warm up" in some crazy way)*

FLUTE: *(talking out loud to himself)* I wonder if the Thisbe could be a boy? No, no, no....it is a love story.

PUCK: The boss said something smelly and vile, huh? *(PUCK puts a sheet over Bottoms head and pulls him offstage)* I will turn this actor into a donkey! And get the boss' Queen to fall in love with him!!!! Hee, hee, hee.

QUINCE (or FLUTE): *(looking around)* Hey Bottom, where are you?

BOTTOM: *(BOTTOM returns with Donkey head)* Okay, I'm ready!

QUINCE & FLUTE: Aghhhhhhhhhhhhhhhhhhhhhhhhh!!!!

(ALL see BOTTOM transformed and freak out screaming and yelling anything and everything as they run off stage. TITANIA wakes at this noise and sees BOTTOM)

BOTTOM: Why do they run away? *(feeling his face)* Hey, I think I need to shave.

TITANIA: What angel wakes me from my flowery bed?

BOTTOM: Hey, where did you come from? And who are you?

TITANIA: I awoke to think you are the best looking person ever! I love thee.

BOTTOM: Whoa! Methinks you should have little reason for that. *(TITANIA grabs BOTTOM'S hand and pulls him off stage)*

ACT 3 SCENE 2

(OBERON enters unseen by all but PUCK)

OBERON: So, have you seen my queen?

PUCK: My mistress with a monster is in love. *(very, very, very happy with himself)*

OBERON: Nice! *(DEMETRIUS chasing HERMIA enter)*

DEMETRIUS: How about now?

HERMIA: No. *(more chasing)*

DEMETRIUS: Now?

HERMIA: No! I do not, nor will not like you! Go away! *(shoves him and runs off stage. DEMETRIUS chases her)*

OBERON: *(to PUCK)* You messed it all up! You put the love potion on the wrong Athenian's eyes.

PUCK: I did? Oh well, *(to audience)* but this is very entertaining!

OBERON: *(serious)* This is a problem. *(points for him to leave)*

PUCK: Are you kidding me? This is great entertainment. Just ask the audience. *(to audience)* Hey audience, don't you think this is great entertainment? *(PUCK gets audience to clap and cheer him on. Meanwhile, lovers chasing is still happening)*

OBERON: PUCK! Do something!

(LYSANDER, HELENA, DEMETRIUS, and HERMIA enter)

PUCK: Fine! FREEZE!

(PUCK throws pixie dust on DEMETRIUS. DEMETRIUS suddenly falls madly in love with HELENA)

PUCK: UNFREEZE!

LYSANDER: O Helen, goddess, nymph, perfect, divine! I love you!

HELENA: What? O spite!

DEMETRIUS: *(DEMETRIUS shoves LYSANDER over)* You love her? No! I love thee more!

(LYSANDER and DEMETRIUS start pushing and fighting each other to be noticed by HELENA)

HELENA: Aghhhhhhhhhhh!

HERMIA: *(Upset off to the side)* You thief of love! You took my guy! You took both of my guys!

HELENA: What did you say earlier? Oh, yeah... Stinks to be you.

HERMIA: Oh, yeah? *(HERMIA chases HELENA off stage. The boys chase HELENA while wrestling with each other. PUCK, again very, very amused at the situation)*

PUCK: Isn't this great!

OBERON: *(very stern)* Puck!

PUCK: I know, I know......*(mocking Oberon)* "This is a problem".

(PUCK pouts, exits chasing foursome)

ACT 4 SCENE 1

(TITANIA and BOTTOM enter)

TITANIA: Can I have my fairy go get you goodies, my sweet love?

BOTTOM: *(Very excited)* Yeah! Have her bring me a candy bar!

OBERON: FREEZE! A donkey, hmmmm. Although this is very funny, I do kind of like her. *(OBERON knocks out BOTTOM, and blows pixie dust on TITANIA'S head)*

OBERON: UNFREEZE!

TITANIA: *(TITANIA awakes like she was in a weird dream)* Oberon, I had a weird dream, you won't believe what happened.

OBERON: Let me guess, you fell in love with a donkey?

TITANIA: *(TITANIA nods her head surprised)* Yeah, how did you know?

OBERON: There lies your love. *(points at BOTTOM)*

TITANIA: Yuck!

OBERON: But you like me now!

TITANIA: Cool! *(TITANIA and OBERON exit)*

(LYSANDER, HELENA, DEMETRIUS, and HERMIA enter, PUCK follows. All are still arguing just like before)

PUCK: FREEZE! *(All four freeze in place. PUCK throws pixie dust on DEMETRIUS and faces him towards Helena. Then he throws pixie dust on LYSANDER and faces him towards HERMIA)*

PUCK: UNFREEZE!

LYSANDER: Hermia, I love you.

HERMIA: About time!

DEMETRIUS: Hey Helena, I love you.

HELENA: Finally!

LYSANDER: Hey, I'm tired. Let's go to sleep.

EVERYBODY: Okay. *(they all fall asleep on the ground. PUCK, a little depressed the fun is over, exits. While he exits, he grabs the donkey head from the sleeping BOTTOM)*

(a small amount of time passes then the lovers wakeup)

LOVERS: It was all a dream.

HERMIA: *(to audience)* Oh no! I have to have an answer for the Duke today; execution, nunnery, or listen to my father? Ohhh.... But, I still love Lysander.

DEMETRIUS: And I love Helena.

LYSANDER: Well then Hermia, your dad may be upset, but I think the Duke will be happy we are all in love, and I am sure he will want us all to get married too! I mean, this is a Shakespeare comedy, right? *(they all nod)* Everybody ALWAYS gets married in a Shakespeare comedy!

LOVERS: Okay! Let's all go get married. *(All exit)*

ACT 4 SCENE 2

(A candy bar flies on stage and hits Bottom.

BOTTOM awakes)

BOTTOM: *(feeling his face)* Methought I was, methought I had....ahhhh never mind. It must have just been a dream!

(QUINCE and FLUTE enters very depressed)

QUINCE (or FLUTE): *(to audience)* Have any of you seen Bottom?

FLUTE: No?

(BOTTOM walks over)

QUINCE and FLUTE: Bottom!

BOTTOM: Guess what? We get to perform our play in front of the Duke!

QUINCE and FLUTE: Yeah! *(All exit)*

ACT 5 SCENE 1

(LYSANDER, HERMIA, HELENA, and DEMETRIUS enter)

DEMETRIUS: The Duke couldn't be here tonight, but he said that we were going to watch a play. Helena, what do we have?

HELENA: *(Reading from paper)* Listen to this, "A tedious brief scene of young Pyramus and his love Thisbe; very tragical mirth". It is called "Pyramus and Thisbe".

EVERYBODY: Yeah! That sounds great! Where's the popcorn?

(QUINCE, FLUTE and BOTTOM enter, and BOTTOM takes center stage)

QUINCE (or BOTTOM): *(announces play to audience in a deep announcer's voice)* Now presenting, 'Pyramus and Thisbe'. *(ALL applause)*

BOTTOM (as Pyramus): I love you, but I can never visit you, so thus die I, thus, thus, thus! Now am I dead. Now die, die, die, die, die. *(PYRAMUS kills himself and dies very, very, very, very dramatically and funny)*

FLUTE (as Thisbe): Asleep my love? What, dead, my dove? I must die too. Adieu, adieu, adieu! *(THISBE kills herself and just falls over. ALL applause while FLUTE and BOTTOM bow and exit)*

LYSANDER: Well they couldn't have died soon enough! Time to go to bed. *(All exit. PUCK enters and addresses audience)*

PUCK: *(to audience)* If we shadows have offended, think but this, and all is mended. In other words, we really hope you enjoyed our dream. So give me your hands, *(starts clapping)* if we be friends. *(claps with audience)* Goodnight! *(PUCK exits waving to the audience)*

THE END

The 10-Minute or so
A Midsummer Night's Dream
By William Shakespeare
Creatively edited by Brendan P. Kelso

11-14+ Actors

CAST OF CHARACTERS:

*EGEUS – Father of Hermia

**THESEUS – Duke of Athens

***HIPPOLYTA – Queen of the Amazons – in love with Theseus

HERMIA – Daughter of Egeus and in love with Lysander

LYSANDER – In love with Hermia

HELENA – In love with Demetrius

DEMETRIUS – Thinks he is in love with Helena

OBERON – King of the Fairies

PUCK – Troublemaker fairy - works for Oberon

TITANIA – Queen of the Fairies

FAIRY – Works for Titania

QUINCE – Leader of the Mechanicals

BOTTOM – Lead actor of the Mechanicals

FLUTE – An actor in the Mechanicals

****MECHANICALS – a group of crazy actors

*Egeus and Fairy can be played by the same actor

**Oberon and Theseus can be played by the same actor

***Hippolyta and Titania can be played by the same actor

****Mechanicals can be extra characters if needed.

ACT 1 SCENE 1

(HIPPOLYTA and THESEUS enter)

HIPPOLYTA: Theseus, are we getting married yet?

THESEUS: No.

HIPPOLYTA: Are we getting married yet? *(said like a whiny kid)*

THESEUS: NO.

HIPPOLYTA: Are we getting married yet?

THESEUS: NOOOOOOOO.

HIPPOLYTA: Sorry, but I am soooo excited!

THESEUS: Only three days left my dear Hippolyta. Look, here comes Egeus.

(EGEUS and HERMIA enter)

EGEUS: *(frustrated)* Duke, Duchess, I am sooooo mad at my daughter, Hermia!

HIPPOLYTA: Why?

EGEUS: She doesn't want to marry Demetrius.

THESEUS: Hmmmm, come here, Hermia.

HIPPOLYTA: *(To Theseus)* Be nice to her.

HERMIA: Yes, sir.

THESEUS: You have three choices: execution, go to a nunnery, or listen to your father. I want an answer before I get married, got it?

HERMIA: Got it. *(THESEUS, HIPPOLYTA, and EGEUS exit)*

HERMIA: Oh .... LYSANDER!!!!! *(LYSANDER enters)*

LYSANDER: What's wrong, Hermia?

HERMIA: My dad wants me to marry Demetrius, bleh...., but I want to marry you, Lysander!

LYSANDER: That's all right, Hermia. The course of true love never did run smooth. We'll run off to my Aunt's house. She lives in a place that is far, far, far away and we will go through the enchanted forest in the middle of the night, and probably get lost!

HERMIA: Sounds great! *(HELENA enters)*

HELENA: *(depressed)* Oh Hermia, Demetrius loves your beauty. Why can't I be hot like you, then maybe he would love my beauty!

HERMIA: Wow, stinks to be you. Hey, want to know a secret?

HELENA: Yeah!

HERMIA: *(as if whispering in her ear)*, Lysander and I are going to run off to his Aunt's house. It's far, far, far away. Promise me you will not tell a single person!

HELENA: Promise! *(HERMIA and LYSANDER exit)* *(To audience)* Hmmmm....I have a better idea, why don't I let Demetrius know of fair Hermia's flight, and then maybe he will fall in love with me! *(HELENA exits)*

ACT 1 SCENE 2

(MECHANICALS enter)

QUINCE: Is all our company here?

MECHANICALS: Yes!

QUINCE: Fabulous! We are going to perform a play before the Duke and Duchess on his wedding day.

MECHANICALS: Yeah!

QUINCE: Our play is 'The most lamentable comedy, and most cruel death of Pyramus and Thisbe', and we shall call it...... "Pyramus and Thisbe".

MECHANICALS: Yeah!

QUINCE: Bottom, you will play Pyramus.

BOTTOM: No, No, No! That's not acceptable! I deserve the best part because I am the best actor!

FLUTE: *(To other mechanicals or audience)* More like OVERactor.

BOTTOM: I heard that. *(glaring at Flute)*

QUINCE: That is the best part. Flute, you will play Thisbe.

FLUTE: *(spoken in a very manly voice)* Great! What is Thisbe? A wandering knight?

QUINCE: No, *she* is the lead female part, and you can talk in a small voice.

FLUTE: What?! Did I hear you right? Let me not play a woman; I have a beard coming.

BOTTOM: Let me play Thisbe too! *(starts acting like a girl)*

QUINCE: No. You already have a part, the best part.

BOTTOM: Yeah, yeah.

QUINCE: That leaves us with Thisbe's mother, the Lion's part, let's see....

BOTTOM: I can play the Lion's part too! Listen to my lion's roar! *(Bottom starts to roar)*

QUINCE: No. No. NO! You would fright the Duchess and the ladies, that they would shriek; and that were enough to hang us all.

BOTTOM: Man, you are tough! *(as MECHANICALS exit FLUTE says his line)*

FLUTE: Do I have to play a girl? This is not good, not good at all. *(all exit)*

ACT 2 SCENE 1

(FAIRY enters dancing across stage and singing to herself. PUCK enters but hides from Fairy)

PUCK: Boo!

FAIRY: Aghhh!!!

PUCK: How now, spirit! Whither wander you?

FAIRY: Hey, don't people call you Puck?

PUCK: *(sarcastic)* A very brilliant observation.

FAIRY: Aren't you that shrewd and knavish sprite call'd Puck? Don't you cause all sorts of trouble? Aren't you a devilish little imp?

PUCK: Yep. That would be me! *(very proud)*

FAIRY: Oh look, here comes Titania, Queen of the Fairies. I work for her.

PUCK: Yeah, well here comes Oberon, King of the Fairies. He's my boss. *(OBERON and TITANIA enter)*

OBERON: *(Rude and sarcastic)* Hello.

TITANIA: Goodbye. *(Just as rude and sarcastic, and wanting to leave in a hurry)*

OBERON: Wait, please, there is something that I would like to tell you.

TITANIA: What?

OBERON: *(in a sing-song voice)* I don't like you!

TITANIA: *(heavy sarcasim)* Boo hoo, boo hoo hoo.

OBERON: If you give me the treasure I asked for, then I will go with thee.

TITANIA: Not a chance. Fairy, let's go! I'm out of here!

FAIRY: Okay.

OBERON: *(mocking TITANIA)* I'm out of here!

TITANIA: Bye bye! *(TITANIA and FAIRY exit)*

OBERON: *(very mad)* AAAAGGGGGHHHHH!!!!!!!!!! I have to do something mean to her! *(talking to himself)* What to do? What to do? What to do?

PUCK: *(with a big grin)* So, how can I help?

OBERON: Go get me the magical purple flower.

PUCK: I'll put a girdle round about the earth in forty minutes. *(PUCK starts to leave)*

OBERON: Huh? *(not understanding what Puck just said)*

PUCK: *(frustrated)* I'll be right back. *(shaking his head and mumbling, PUCK exits)*

(HELENA and DEMETRIUS enter. OBERON watches, unseen)

DEMETRIUS: I love thee not, therefore pursue me not.

HELENA: Demetrius, don't you love me?

DEMETRIUS: No, you bug me, Helena.

HELENA: Even though I told you about Hermia and Lysander running off together?

DEMETRIUS: You still bug me. Now leave me alone... *(shoves HELENA away)*

HELENA: Demetrius, the more you hate me, the more I will love you!

DEMETRIUS: Aghhhhh! Leave me alone! *(HELENA chases DEMETRIUS offstage. PUCK enters)*

PUCK: Your fairy has returned with the magical purple flower!

OBERON: I pray thee, give it me. *(PUCK hands the flower to OBERON)* This is a love potion. I'm going to put some on Titania's eyes. Then she will awake and fall in love with the first thing she sees, hopefully something filthy and smelly! Puck, you go do something constructive.

PUCK: Constructive?

OBERON: *(frustrated)* I saw a young Athenian couple mad at each other. Use this flower and make them fall in love.

PUCK: Okay. *(PUCK exits. OBERON hides behind a tree)*

ACT 2 SCENE 2

(TITANIA enters with FAIRY)

TITANIA: Wow, I'm tired. I think I will fall asleep in the middle of this dark and enchanted forest, while my husband is very, very mad at me. Fairy!

FAIRY: Yes?

TITANIA: I want you to sing me to sleep.

FAIRY: Sing?

TITANIA: Yes, sing.

FAIRY: Ahhhh okay......la, la, te da...... la, la, te da...... la, la, te da......la *(TITANIA falls quickly to sleep)*

FAIRY: Okay. Sleep tight! *(Once the FAIRY notices Titania is asleep the FAIRY sees a bunch of flies and tries to catch them, and chase them off stage.)*

OBERON: Well, well, well, looky here! *(OBERON, places potion on TITANIA'S eyes)* Wake when some vile thing is near! *(OBERON exits)*

(LYSANDER and HERMIA enter)

LYSANDER: Hmmm, these trees look familiar.

HERMIA: What do you mean by that?

LYSANDER: I have forgot our way.

HERMIA: That's okay. I'm tired. Let's go to sleep.

LYSANDER: Okay. *(LYSANDER and HERMIA lie down and go to sleep)*

PUCK: *(PUCK enters and sees LYSANDER lying on ground)* An Athenian couple, just like the boss said! Pretty soul, how can he be mad at her? A little on each eye and poof, you will now fall in love with the first thing you see! *(places potion on LYSANDER'S eyes. PUCK stands back to watch)*

(DEMETRIUS and HELENA enter)

DEMETRIUS: You are still annoying me, you're like my dog.

HELENA: Then let me be your pet and I will follow you everywhere. *(howls with excitment)*

DEMETRIUS: Noooooo! Hey, look at that *(points at something off stage in opposite direction)* I'm outta here! *(DEMETRIUS exits)*

HELENA: Aghhhh *(Sees LYSANDER lying on ground, wakes him)* Lysander? Lysander, if you live, good sir, awake. *(HELENA kicks LYSANDER)* I said AWAKE!

LYSANDER: What? *(LYSANDER wakes up totally in love with Helena)*

HELENA: I think Demetrius does not love me.

LYSANDER: And run through fire I will for thy sweet sake.

HELENA: Huh?

LYSANDER: I love you!

HELENA: *(very matter of fact)* But you love Hermia.

LYSANDER: Not Hermia, but Helena I love: Who would not change a raven for a dove? *(Chasing her, trying to hug and kiss her)* Oh kiss me darling!

HELENA: Aghhhhhhhhh! *(HELENA screaming runs off, LYSANDER chases her)*

(HERMIA wakes up, confused)

HERMIA: Hello? Lysander? Where did you go? *(HERMIA exits. PUCK is very amused with the situation)*

ACT 3 SCENE 1

(MECHANICALS enter. PUCK is excited that there are new people to watch)

QUINCE: Are we all met?

BOTTOM: There are some lines that I think we need to change in the script.

QUINCE: No, we need to rehearse.

BOTTOM: Okay, I need to warm up first. *(BOTTOM moves over to the side of the stage to "warm up" in some crazy way)*

FLUTE: Can we talk about this girl part?

QUINCE: Would you just come over here and work on your lines? *(MECHANICALS rehearse together, saying the words "rehearse" several times quietly)*

PUCK: Something smelly, huh? *(PUCK puts a sheet over Bottoms head and pulls him offstage)* I will turn this actor into a donkey! And get the boss' Queen to fall in love with him!!!! Hee, hee, hee.

BOTTOM: *(BOTTOM returns with Donkey head)* Okay, I'm ready!

EVERYBODY: Aghhhhhhhhhhhhhhhhhhhhhhhhhhhhhhhhh!!!!

(The MECHANICALS see BOTTOM transformed and freak out screaming and yelling anything and everything as they run off stage. TITANIA wakes at this noise and sees BOTTOM)

BOTTOM: Why do they run away? *(feeling his face)* Hey, I think I need to shave.

TITANIA: What angel wakes me from my flowery bed?

BOTTOM: Hey, where did you come from? And who are you?

TITANIA: I awoke to think you are the best looking person ever! I love thee.

BOTTOM: Whoa! Methinks you should have little reason for that. *(TITANIA grabs BOTTOM'S hand and pulls him off stage)*

ACT 3 SCENE 2

(OBERON enters unseen by all but PUCK)

OBERON: So, have you seen my queen?

PUCK: My mistress with a monster is in love. *(very, very, very happy with himself)*

OBERON: Nice! *(DEMETRIUS chasing HERMIA enter)*

DEMETRIUS: How about now?

HERMIA: No. *(more chasing)*

DEMETRIUS: Now?

HERMIA: No! I do not, nor will not like you! Go away! *(shoves him and runs off stage. DEMETRIUS chases her)*

OBERON: *(to PUCK)* You messed it all up! You put the love potion on the wrong Athenian's eyes.

PUCK: I did? Oh well, *(to audience)* but this is very entertaining!

OBERON: *(serious)* This is a problem. *(points for him to leave)*

PUCK: Are you kidding me? This is great entertainment. Just ask the audience. *(to audience)* Hey audience, don't you think this is great entertainment? *(PUCK gets audience to clap and cheer him on. Meanwhile, lovers chasing is still happening)*

OBERON: PUCK! Do something!

(LYSANDER, HELENA, DEMETRIUS, and HERMIA enter)

PUCK: Fine! FREEZE!

(PUCK throws pixie dust on DEMETRIUS. DEMETRIUS suddenly falls madly in love with HELENA)

PUCK: UNFREEZE!

LYSANDER: O Helen, goddess, nymph, perfect, divine! I love you!

HELENA: What? O spite!

DEMETRIUS: *(DEMETRIUS shoves LYSANDER over)* You love her? No! I love thee more!

(LYSANDER and DEMETRIUS start pushing and fighting each other to be noticed by HELENA)

HELENA: Aghhhhhhhhhhh!

HERMIA: *(Upset off to the side)* You thief of love! You took my guy! You took both of my guys!

HELENA: What did you say earlier? Oh, yeah... stinks to be you.

HERMIA: Oh, yeah? *(HERMIA chases HELENA off stage. The boys chase HELENA while wrestling with each other. PUCK, again very, very amused at the situation)*

PUCK: Isn't this great!

OBERON: *(very stern)* Puck!

PUCK: I know, I know......*(mocking OBERON)* "This is a problem". *(PUCK pouts, exits chasing foursome)*

ACT 4 SCENE 1

(TITANIA, BOTTOM, and FAIRY enter)

TITANIA: Can I have my fairy go get you goodies, my sweet love?

BOTTOM: Yeah! *(to FAIRY)* Go get me a candy bar! *(FAIRY exits mumbling)*

OBERON: FREEZE! A donkey, hmmmm. Although this is very funny, I do kind of like her. *(OBERON knocks out BOTTOM, and blows pixie dust on TITANIA'S head)*

OBERON: UNFREEZE!

TITANIA: *(TITANIA awakes like she was in a weird dream)* Oberon, I had a weird dream, you won't believe what happened.

OBERON: Let me guess, you fell in love with a donkey? There lies your love. *(points at BOTTOM)*

TITANIA: Yuck!

OBERON: But you like me now!

TITANIA: Cool! *(TITANIA and OBERON exit)*

(LYSANDER, HELENA, DEMETRIUS, and HERMIA enter, PUCK follows. All are still arguing just like before)

PUCK: FREEZE! *(All four freeze in place. PUCK throws pixie dust on DEMETRIUS and faces him towards Helena. Then he throws pixie dust on LYSANDER and faces him towards HERMIA)*

PUCK: UNFREEZE!

LYSANDER: Hermia, I love you.

HERMIA: About time!

DEMETRIUS: Hey Helena, I love you.

HELENA: Finally!

LYSANDER: Hey, I'm tired. Let's go to sleep.

EVERYBODY: Okay. *(They all fall asleep on the ground. PUCK, a little depressed the fun is over, exits. While he exits, he grabs the donkey head from the sleeping BOTTOM)*

(THESEUS, EGEUS enter)

EGEUS: Aghhhhhhhhh! My lord, this is my daughter here asleep!

THESEUS: Yeah, next to some dude and two other Athenians.

EGEUS: Yeah, the wrong dude!

THESEUS: Wake them.

EGEUS: *(EGEUS wakes them)* Hello! What are you doing hanging out with this guy?

LOVERS: It was all a dream.

EGEUS: Yeah, right.

THESEUS: Hermia, do you have your answer? Is it execution, nunnery, or listen to your father?

HERMIA: I still love Lysander.

DEMETRIUS: And I love Helena.

EGEUS: Aghhhhhhhh! *(EGEUS runs off stage in a mad fervor)*

THESEUS: This is great! Let's all go get married.

LOVERS: What?

THESEUS: I mean, this is a Shakespeare comedy, right? *(they all nod)* Everybody ALWAYS gets married in a Shakespeare comedy!

LOVERS: Okay! *(All exit)*

ACT 4 SCENE 2

(A candy bar flies on stage and hits BOTTOM. BOTTOM awakes)

BOTTOM: *(feeling his face)* Methought I was, methought I had....ahhhh never mind. It must have just been a dream!

(MECHANICALS enter – depressed)

QUINCE: Has anyone seen Bottom?

FLUTE: No.

QUINCE: *(Down center asking audience members)* Have any of you seen Bottom?

(BOTTOM walks over)

MECHANICALS: Bottom!

BOTTOM: Guess what? We get to perform our play in front of the Duke!

MECHANICALS: Yeah! *(All exit)*

ACT 5 SCENE 1

(THESEUS, HIPPOLYTA, EGEUS, LYSANDER, HERMIA, HELENA, and DEMETRIUS enter)

THESEUS: Before our nuptials, we are going to watch a play. Hippolyta, what do we have?

HIPPOLYTA: *(Reading from paper)* Listen to this: "A tedious brief scene of young Pyramus and his love Thisbe; very tragical mirth". It is called "Pyramus and Thisbe".

EVERYBODY: Yeah! That sounds great! Where's the popcorn?

THESEUS: *(Yelling off stage)* Bring on the Mechanicals!

(MECHANICALS enter, and QUINCE takes center stage)

QUINCE: *(announces play to audience in a deep announcer's voice)* Now presenting 'Pyramus and Thisbe'. *(All applause, and QUINCE sits down to side)*

EGEUS: *(Talking to THESEUS)* I just love their costumes.

BOTTOM (as Pyramus): I love you, but I can never visit you, so thus die I, thus, thus, thus! Now am I dead. Now die, die, die, die, die. *(PYRAMUS kills himself and dies very, very, very, very dramatically and funny)*

FLUTE (as Thisbe): Asleep my love? What, dead, my dove? I must die too. Adieu, adieu, adieu! *(THISBE kills herself and just falls over. All applause while MECHANICALS bow and exit)*

THESEUS: Well they couldn't have died soon enough! Time to go to bed. *(All exit. PUCK enters and addresses audience)*

PUCK: *(to audience)* If we shadows have offended, think but this, and all is mended. In other words, we really hope you enjoyed our dream. So give me your hands, if we be friends. *(claps with audience)* Goodnight! *(PUCK exits waving to audience)*

THE END

The 10-Minute or so
A Midsummer Night's Dream
By William Shakespeare
Creatively edited by Brendan P. Kelso
15-20+ Actors

CAST OF CHARACTERS:

***EGEUS** – Father of Hermia

****THESEUS** – Duke of Athens

*****HIPPOLYTA** – Queen of the Amazons – in love with Theseus

HERMIA – Daughter of Egeus and in love with Lysander

LYSANDER – In love with Hermia

HELENA – In love with Demetrius

DEMETRIUS – Thinks he is in love with Helena

OBERON – King of the Fairies

PUCK – Troublemaker fairy - works for Oberon

TITANIA – Queen of the Fairies

*******PEASEBLOSSOM** – Fairy, works for Titania

*******COBWEB** – Fairy, works for Titania

*******MOTH** – Fairy, works for Titania

*******MUSTARDSEED** – Fairy, works for Titania

QUINCE – Leader of the Mechanicals

BOTTOM – Lead actor of the Mechanicals

FLUTE – An actor in the Mechanicals

******SNOUT** – An actor in the Mechanicals

******STARVELING** – An actor in the Mechanicals

******SNUG** – An actor in the Mechanicals

*Egeus and Fairy can be played by the same actor

**Theseus and Oberon can be played by the same actor

***Hippolyta and Titania can be played by the same actor

****Snout, Starveling, and Snug's lines can be moved to other Mechanicals to accommodate for number of actors.

*****Fairy lines can be combined to one or more fairies to accommodate for number of actors.

ACT 1 SCENE 1

(HIPPOLYTA and THESEUS enter)

HIPPOLYTA: Theseus, are we getting married yet?

THESEUS: No.

HIPPOLYTA: Are we getting married yet? *(said like a whiny kid)*

THESEUS: NO.

HIPPOLYTA: Are we getting married yet?

THESEUS: NOOOOOOOOO.

HIPPOLYTA: Sorry, but I am soooo excited!

THESEUS: Only three days left, my dear Hippolyta. Look, here comes Egeus.

(EGEUS and HERMIA enter)

EGEUS: *(frustrated)* Duke, Duchess, I am sooooo mad at my daughter, Hermia!

HIPPOLYTA: Why?

EGEUS: She doesn't want to marry Demetrius.

THESEUS: Hmmmm, come here, Hermia.

HIPPOLYTA: *(To Theseus)* Be nice to her.

HERMIA: Yes, sir.

THESEUS: You have three choices: execution, go to a nunnery, or listen to your father. I want an answer before I get married, got it?

HERMIA: Got it. *(THESEUS, HIPPOLYTA, and EGEUS exit)*

HERMIA: Oh .... LYSANDER!!!!! *(LYSANDER enters)*

LYSANDER: What's wrong, Hermia?

HERMIA: My dad wants me to marry Demetrius, bleh...., but I want to marry you, Lysander!

LYSANDER: That's all right, Hermia. The course of true love never did run smooth. We'll run off to my Aunt's house. She lives in a place that is far, far, far away and we will go through the enchanted forest in the middle of the night, and probably get lost!

HERMIA: Sounds great! *(HELENA enters)*

HELENA: *(depressed)* Oh Hermia, Demetrius loves your beauty. Why can't I be hot like you, then maybe he would love my beauty!

HERMIA: Wow, stinks to be you. Hey, want to know a secret?

HELENA: Yeah!

HERMIA: *(as if whispering in her ear)* Lysander and I are going to run off to his Aunt's house. It's far, far, far away. Promise me you will not tell a single person!

HELENA: Promise! *(HERMIA and LYSANDER exit)* *(To audience)* Hmmmm....I have a better idea, why don't I let Demetrius know of fair Hermia's flight, and then maybe he will fall in love with me!

(HELENA exits)

(MECHANICALS enter)

QUINCE: Is all our company here?

MECHANICALS: Yes!

QUINCE: Fabulous! We are going to perform a play before the Duke and Duchess on his wedding day.

MECHANICALS: Yeah!

QUINCE: Our play is 'The most lamentable comedy, and most cruel death of Pyramus and Thisbe', and we shall call it...... "Pyramus and Thisbe".

MECHANICALS: Yeah!

QUINCE: Bottom, you will play Pyramus.

BOTTOM: No, No, No! That's not acceptable! I deserve the best part because I am the best actor!

FLUTE: *(To other mechanicals or audience)* More like OVERactor.

BOTTOM: I heard that. *(glaring at Flute)*

QUINCE: That is the best part. Flute, you will play Thisbe.

FLUTE: *(spoken in a very manly voice)* Great! What is Thisbe? A wandering knight?

QUINCE: No, *she* is the lead female part, and you can talk in a small voice.

FLUTE: What?! Did I hear you right? Let me not play a woman; I have a beard coming.

BOTTOM: Let me play Thisbe too! *(starts acting like a girl)*

QUINCE: No. You already have a part, the best part.

BOTTOM: Yeah, yeah.

QUINCE: Starveling?

STARVELING: Here, Peter Quince.

QUINCE: Starveling, you must play Thisbe's mother.

STARVELING: Huh? I have to play a girl too?

QUINCE: Tom Snout?

SNOUT: Here, Peter Quince.

QUINCE: You, Pyramus' father. Snug?

SNUG: Here, Peter Quince.

QUINCE: You the Lion's part, and I hope here is a play fitted for the Duke!

SNUG: Ahhh Quince?

QUINCE: *(impatiently)* Yes.

SNUG: I am slow of study, do you have the script?

QUINCE: Snug, listen buddy, it is nothing but roaring. You will be fine. *(BOTTOM pushes SNUG away)*

BOTTOM: I can play the Lion's part too! Listen to my lion's roar! *(Bottom starts to roar)*

QUINCE: No. No. NO! You would fright the Duchess and the ladies, that they would shriek; and that were enough to hang us all.

MECHANICALS: That would hang us!

BOTTOM: Man, you are tough! *(as MECHANICALS exit FLUTE and STARVELING say their line)*

FLUTE & STARVELING: Do we have to play girls? *(all exit)*

ACT 2 SCENE 1

(FAIRIES enter dancing across stage and singing to themselves. PUCK enters but hides from FAIRIES)

PUCK: Boo!

FAIRIES: Aghhh!!!

PUCK: How now, spirit! Whither wander you?

PEASEBLOSSOM: Hey, don't people call you Puck?

PUCK: *(sarcastic)* A very brilliant observation.

COBWEB: Aren't you that shrewd and knavish sprite call'd Puck? Don't you cause all sorts of trouble? Aren't you a devilish little imp?

PUCK: Yep. That would be me! *(very proud)*

MOTH: The one that frights the maidens of the villagery?

PUCK: Again, yes!

MUSTARDSEED: Oh look, here comes Titania, Queen of the Fairies. We work for her.

PUCK: Yeah, well here comes Oberon, King of the Fairies. He's my boss. *(OBERON and TITANIA enter)*

OBERON: *(Rude and sarcastic)* Hello.

TITANIA: Goodbye. *(Just as rude and sarcastic, and wanting to leave in a hurry)*

OBERON: Wait, please, there is something that I would like to tell you.

TITANIA: What?

OBERON: *(in a sing-song voice)* I don't like you!

TITANIA: *(heavy sarcasim)* Boo hoo, boo hoo hoo.

OBERON: If you give me the treasure I asked for, then I will go with thee.

TITANIA: Not a chance. Fairies, let's go! I'm out of here!

FAIRIES: Okay.

OBERON: *(mocking TITANIA)* I'm out of here!

TITANIA: Bye bye! *(TITANIA and FAIRIES exit)*

OBERON: *(very mad)* AAAAGGGGGHHHHH!!!!!!!!! I have to do something mean to her! *(talking to himself)* What to do? What to do? What to do?

PUCK: *(with a big grin)* So, how can I help?

OBERON: Go get me the magical purple flower.

PUCK: I'll put a girdle round about the earth in forty minutes. *(PUCK starts to leave)*

OBERON: Huh? *(not understanding what Puck just said)*

PUCK: *(frustrated)* I'll be right back. *(shaking his head and mumbling, PUCK exits)*

(HELENA and DEMETRIUS enter. OBERON watches, unseen)

DEMETRIUS: I love thee not, therefore pursue me not.

HELENA: Demetrius, don't you love me?

DEMETRIUS: No, you bug me, Helena.

HELENA: Even though I told you about Hermia and Lysander running off together?

DEMETRIUS: You still bug me. Now leave me alone... *(shoves HELENA away)*

HELENA: Demetrius, the more you hate me, the more I will love you!

DEMETRIUS: Aghhhhh! Leave me alone! *(HELENA chases DEMETRIUS offstage. PUCK enters)*

PUCK: Your fairy has returned with the magical purple flower!

OBERON: I pray thee, give it me. *(PUCK hands the flower to OBERON)* This is a love potion. I'm going to put some on Titania's eyes. Then she will awake and fall in love with the first thing she sees, hopefully something filthy and smelly! Puck, you go do something constructive.

PUCK: Constructive?

OBERON: *(frustrated)* I saw a young Athenian couple mad at each other. Use this flower and make them fall in love.

PUCK: Okay. *(PUCK exits. OBERON hides behind a tree)*

ACT 2 SCENE 2

(TITANIA enters with FAIRIES)

TITANIA: Wow, I'm tired. I think I will fall asleep in the middle of this dark and enchanted forest, while my husband is very, very mad at me. Fairies!

FAIRIES: Yes?

TITANIA: I want you to sing me to sleep.

FAIRIES: Sing?

TITANIA: Yes, sing.

FAIRIES: Ahhhh okay.......la, la, te da...... la, la, te da...... la, la, te da......la *(TITANIA falls quickly to sleep)*

FAIRIES: Okay. Sleep tight! *(Once the FAIRIES notice Titania is asleep they see a bunch of flies and try to catch them, and chase them off stage.)*

OBERON: Well, well, well, looky here! *(OBERON, places potion on TITANIA'S eyes)* Wake when some vile thing is near! *(OBERON exits)*

(LYSANDER and HERMIA enter)

LYSANDER: Hmmm, these trees look familiar.

HERMIA: What do you mean by that?

LYSANDER: I have forgot our way.

HERMIA: That's okay. I'm tired. Let's go to sleep.

LYSANDER: Okay. *(LYSANDER and HERMIA lie down and go to sleep)*

PUCK: *(PUCK enters and sees LYSANDER lying on ground)* An Athenian couple, just like the boss said! Pretty soul, how can he be mad at her? A little on each eye and poof, you will now fall in love with the first thing you see! *(places potion on LYSANDER'S eyes. PUCK stands back to watch)*

(DEMETRIUS and HELENA enter running)

DEMETRIUS: You are still annoying me, you're like my dog.

HELENA: Then let me be your pet and I will follow you everywhere. *(howls with excitment)*

DEMETRIUS: Noooooo! Hey, look at that *(points at something off stage in opposite direction)* I'm outta here! *(DEMETRIUS exits)*

HELENA: Aghhhh *(Sees LYSANDER lying on ground, wakes him)* Lysander? Lysander, if you live, good sir, awake. *(HELENA kicks LYSANDER)* I said AWAKE!

LYSANDER: What? *(LYSANDER wakes up totally in love with Helena)*

HELENA: I think Demetrius does not love me.

LYSANDER: And run through fire I will for thy sweet sake.

HELENA: Huh?

LYSANDER: I love you!

HELENA: *(very matter of fact)* But you love Hermia.

LYSANDER: Not Hermia, but Helena I love: Who would not change a raven for a dove? *(Chasing her, trying to hug and kiss her)* Oh kiss me darling!

HELENA: Aghhhhhhhhh! *(HELENA screaming runs off, LYSANDER chases her)*

(HERMIA wakes up, confused)

HERMIA: Hello? Lysander? Where did you go? *(HERMIA exits. PUCK is very amused with the situation)*

ACT 3 SCENE 1

(MECHANICALS enter. PUCK is excited that there are new people to watch)

QUINCE: Are we all met?

BOTTOM: There are some lines that I think we need to change in the script.

QUINCE: No, we need to rehearse.

BOTTOM: Okay, I need to warm up first. *(BOTTOM moves over to the side of the stage to "warm up" in some crazy way)*

FLUTE: Can we talk about this girl part?

STARVELING: Yeah!

QUINCE: Would you just come over here and work on your lines? *(MECHANICALS rehearse together, saying the words "rehearse" several times quietly)*

PUCK: Something smelly, huh? *(PUCK puts a sheet over Bottoms head and pulls him offstage)* I will turn this actor into a donkey! And get the boss' Queen to fall in love with him!!!! Hee, hee, hee.

BOTTOM: *(BOTTOM returns with Donkey head)* Okay, I'm ready!

EVERYBODY: Aghhhhhhhhhhhhhhhhhhhhhhhhhhhhh!!!!

(The MECHANICALS see BOTTOM transformed and freak out screaming and yelling anything and everything as they run off stage. TITANIA wakes at this noise and sees BOTTOM)

BOTTOM: Why do they run away? *(feeling his face)* Hey, I think I need to shave.

TITANIA: What angel wakes me from my flowery bed?

BOTTOM: Hey, where did you come from? And who are you?

TITANIA: I awoke to think you are the best looking person ever! I love thee.

BOTTOM: Whoa! Methinks you should have little reason for that. *(TITANIA grabs BOTTOM'S hand and pulls him off stage)*

ACT 3 SCENE 2

(OBERON enters unseen by all but PUCK)

OBERON: So, have you seen my queen?

PUCK: My mistress with a monster is in love. *(very, very, very happy with himself)*

OBERON: Nice! *(DEMETRIUS chasing HERMIA enter)*

DEMETRIUS: How about now?

HERMIA: No. *(more chasing)*

DEMETRIUS: Now?

HERMIA: No! I do not, nor will not like you! Go away! *(shoves him and runs off stage. DEMETRIUS chases her)*

OBERON: *(to PUCK)* You messed it all up! You put the love potion on the wrong Athenian's eyes.

PUCK: I did? Oh well, *(to audience)* but this is very entertaining!

OBERON: *(serious)* This is a problem. *(points for him to leave)*

PUCK: Are you kidding me? This is great entertainment. Just ask the audience. *(to audience)* Hey audience, don't you think this is great entertainment? *(PUCK gets audience to clap and cheer him on. Meanwhile, lovers chasing is still happening)*

OBERON: PUCK! Do something!

(LYSANDER, HELENA, DEMETRIUS, and HERMIA enter)

PUCK: Fine! FREEZE!

(PUCK throws pixie dust on DEMETRIUS. DEMETRIUS suddenly falls madly in love with HELENA)

PUCK: UNFREEZE!

LYSANDER: O Helen, goddess, nymph, perfect, divine! I love you!

HELENA: What? O spite!

DEMETRIUS: *(DEMETRIUS shoves LYSANDER over)* You love her? No! I love thee more!

(LYSANDER and DEMETRIUS start pushing and fighting each other to be noticed by HELENA)

HELENA: Aghhhhhhhhhhh!

HERMIA: *(Upset off to the side)* You thief of love! You took my guy! You took both of my guys!

HELENA: What did you say earlier? Oh, yeah... stinks to be you.

HERMIA: Oh, yeah? *(HERMIA chases HELENA off stage. The boys chase HELENA while wrestling with each other. PUCK, again very, very amused at the situation)*

PUCK: Isn't this great!

OBERON: *(very stern)* Puck!

PUCK: I know, I know.......*(mocking OBERON)* "This is a problem". *(PUCK pouts, exits chasing foursome)*

ACT 4 SCENE 1

(TITANIA, BOTTOM, and FARIES enter)

TITANIA: Can I have my fairies go get you goodies, my sweet love?

BOTTOM: Yeah! *(to the FARIES)* Go get me a candy bar! *(FARIES exit mumbling)*

OBERON: FREEZE! A donkey, hmmmm. Although this is very funny, I do kind of like her. *(OBERON nocks out BOTTOM, and blows pixie dust on TITANIA'S head)*

OBERON: UNFREEZE!

TITANIA: *(TITANIA awakes like she was in a weird dream)* Oberon, I had a weird dream, you won't believe what happened.

OBERON: Let me guess, you fell in love with a donkey? There lies your love. *(points at BOTTOM)*

TITANIA: Yuck!

OBERON: But you like me now!

TITANIA: Cool! *(TITANIA and OBERON exit)*

(LYSANDER, HELENA, DEMETRIUS, and HERMIA enter, PUCK follows. All are still arguing just like before)

PUCK: FREEZE! *(All four freeze in place. PUCK throws pixie dust on DEMETRIUS and faces him towards Helena. Then he throws pixie dust on LYSANDER and faces him towards HERMIA)*

PUCK: UNFREEZE!

LYSANDER: Hermia, I love you.

HERMIA: About time!

DEMETRIUS: Hey Helena, I love you.

HELENA: Finally!

LYSANDER: Hey, I'm tired. Let's go to sleep.

EVERYBODY: Okay. *(They all fall asleep on the ground. PUCK, a little depressed the fun is over, exits. While he exits, he grabs the donkey head from the sleeping BOTTOM)*

(THESEUS, EGEUS enter)

EGEUS: Aghhhhhhhhh! My lord, this is my daughter here asleep!

THESEUS: Yeah, next to some dude and two other Athenians.

EGEUS: Yeah, the wrong dude!

THESEUS: Wake them.

EGEUS: *(EGEUS wakes them)* Hello! What are you doing hanging out with this guy?

LOVERS: It was all a dream.

EGEUS: Yeah, right.

THESEUS: Hermia, do you have your answer? Is it execution, nunnery, or listen to your father?

HERMIA: I still love Lysander.

DEMETRIUS: And I love Helena.

EGEUS: Aghhhhhhhh! *(EGEUS runs off stage in a mad fervor)*

THESEUS: This is great! Let's all go get married.

LOVERS: What?

THESEUS: I mean, this is a Shakespeare comedy, right? *(they all nod)* Everybody ALWAYS gets married in a Shakespeare comedy!

LOVERS: Okay! *(All exit)*

ACT 4 SCENE 2

(A candy bar flies on stage and hits BOTTOM. BOTTOM awakes)

BOTTOM: *(feeling his face)* Methought I was, methought I had....ahhhh never mind. It must have just been a dream!

(MECHANICALS enter – depressed)

QUINCE: Has anyone seen Bottom?

MECHANICALS: No.

QUINCE: *(Down center asking audience members)* Have any of you seen Bottom?

(BOTTOM walks over)

MECHANICALS: Bottom!

BOTTOM: Guess what? We get to perform our play in front of the Duke!

MECHANICALS: Yeah! *(All exit)*

ACT 5 SCENE 1

(THESEUS, HIPPOLYTA, EGEUS, LYSANDER, HERMIA, HELENA, and DEMETRIUS enter)

THESEUS: Before our nuptials, we are going to watch a play. Hippolyta, what do we have?

HIPPOLYTA: *(Reading from paper)* Listen to this: "A tedious brief scene of young Pyramus and his love Thisbe; very tragical mirth". It is called "Pyramus and Thisbe".

EVERYBODY: Yeah! That sounds great! Where's the popcorn?

THESEUS: *(Yelling off stage)* Bring on the Mechanicals!

(MECHANICALS enter, and QUINCE takes center stage)

QUINCE: *(announces play to audience in a deep announcer's voice)* Now presenting, 'Pyramus and Thisbe'. *(All applause, and QUINCE sits down to side)*

EGEUS: *(Talking to THESEUS)* I just love their costumes.

BOTTOM (as Pyramus): I love you, but I can never visit you, so thus die I, thus, thus, thus! Now am I dead. Now die, die, die, die, die. *(PYRAMUS kills himself and dies very, very, very, very dramatically and funny)*

FLUTE (as Thisbe): Asleep my love? What, dead, my dove? I must die too. Adieu, adieu, adieu! *(THISBE kills herself and just falls over. All applause while MECHANICALS bow and exit)*

THESEUS: Well they couldn't have died soon enough! Time to go to bed. *(All exit. PUCK enters and addresses audience)*

PUCK: *(to audience)* If we shadows have offended, think but this, and all is mended. In other words, we really hope you enjoyed our dream. So give me your hands, if we be friends. *(claps with audience)* Goodnight! *(PUCK exits waving to audience)*

THE END

Notes

CPSIA information can be obtained at www.ICGtesting.com
Printed in the USA
LVOW04s1917050315

429416LV00011B/97/P